LOOKING AT PAINTINGS

Flowers

The White Heron, 1918–20
Joseph Stella, American (1877–1946)

Looking at Paintings

Flowers

Peggy Roalf

Series Editor
Jacques Lowe

Design
Joseph Guglietti and Steve Kalalian

Belitha Press
London

A
JACQUES LOWE
VISUAL ARTS PROJECTS
BOOK

First published in the United States by Hyperion Books for Children

Printed in Italy

First published in 1994 in the United Kingdom by

 Belitha Press Ltd

31 Newington Green, London N16 9PU

Cataloguing-in-print data available from the British Library

ISBN 1 85561 315 8

Original design concept by Amy Hill
UK Editor: Jill Laidlaw

Contents

Introduction   7

SPRING
Giuseppe Arcimboldo   8

*A YOUNG DAUGHTER OF
THE PICTS*
Jacques Le Moyne de Morgues   10

*FLOWERS, ANIMALS, AND
INSECTS*
Abraham Mignon   12

EGRET AND MALLOW PLANTS
Yamamoto Baiitsu   14

SPRING BOUQUET
Pierre-Auguste Renoir   16

*PINKS AND CLEMATIS IN
A CRYSTAL VASE*
Edouard Manet   18

WILD ROSES AND IRISES
John La Farge   20

SUNFLOWERS
Vincent van Gogh   22

BLUE LILY
Piet Mondrian   24

PORTRAIT OF MÄDA PRIMAVESI
Gustav Klimt   26

BLUE WATER LILIES
Claude Monet   28

NIGHT FLOWERS
Paul Klee   30

WHITE SWEET PEAS
Georgia O'Keeffe   32

GERANIUM
Charles Sheeler   34

THE PURPLE ROBE
Henri Matisse   36

THE FLOWER VENDOR
Diego Rivera   38

THE FLOWER BARGE
André Bauchant   40

THE WRESTLERS' TOMB
René Magritte   42

CAMELLIAS
Robert Kushner   44

Glossary and Index   46-47
Credits   48

To Barbara and Bob Kreminski, with love

Introduction

LOOKING AT PAINTINGS is a series of books about understanding how great artists see when they paint. Painters have been fascinated by flowers since ancient times. However, it was not until the sixteenth century, when new flowers were brought to Europe from the New World and the Far East, that flowers became a major subject in Western art. In *Spring* (page 9), a **symbolic** portrait made out of blossoms and leaves, Giuseppe Arcimboldo expresses nature's importance in life. One hundred years later, the Dutch painter Abraham Mignon painted the endless cycle of birth, growth, death, and rebirth in the intimate woodland scene *Flowers, Animals, and Insects* (page 13).

Western painters discovered the art of the Far East in the middle of the nineteenth century, when Japan opened its doors to trade. The beauty and harmony of Japanese painting influenced artists such as John La Farge in *Wild Roses and Irises* (page 21), Vincent van Gogh in *Sunflowers* (page 23), and Claude Monet in *Blue Water Lilies* (page 29).

Many twentieth-century painters have stated their values and beliefs through flower paintings. Diego Rivera portrayed an **Aztec** farm woman to celebrate his Mexican heritage in *The Flower Vendor* (page 39). Georgia O'Keeffe enlarged the fragile petals of a sweet pea to express the importance of nature in her life. The enormous rose in René Magritte's *The Wrestlers' Tomb* (page 43) tells us to use our dreams in order to understand reality.

Whether you look at a formal garden, a meadow, or your own back garden, you can find inspiration in flowers when you try to see with the eyes of a painter.

Note: words in **bold** are explained in the glossary on pages 46-47.

SPRING, 1573, Giuseppe Arcimboldo
Italian (1527–93), oil on canvas, 73 x 62 cm

Giuseppe Arcimboldo lived during the **Renaissance**, a time when the literature and art of Ancient Greece was reborn in a flowering of the arts, literature, and science all over western Europe. Arcimboldo believed that all living things—humans, plants and animals—were perfectly balanced in a natural scheme that ran like clockwork.

The four seasons

Arcimboldo painted a series of paintings of the four seasons in a unique style. He symbolized spring as the sunlight and air that bring new growth after winter in this portrait made out of of interlocking flowers and leaves. Using a technique called *trompe l'oeil*, Arcimboldo

Arcimboldo's eye for detail and fine brushwork make these flowers look lifelike (detail).

fools our eyes into believing that these flowers, which are painted on a flat, two-dimensional surface are really three-dimensional. Arcimboldo also tricks the viewer into seeing the flowers as a young woman's face and clothing. He painted her skin as pale flowers, her nose as a lily bud, and her dress out of leaves.

Paint made of gold

Although this painting was created more than three hundred years ago, the flowers seem as fresh as spring itself because Arcimboldo used the best and most expensive **colours**, including kermes red made from Far Eastern insects and paint made out of gold. He worked with fine brushes to make each flower stand out as a unique specimen.

A YOUNG DAUGHTER OF THE PICTS, about 1585
Jacques Le Moyne de Morgues, French (c. 1533–88),
water-colour and **gouache** on **vellum**, 25 x 17.5 cm

*E*arly explorers of the New World (North, South and Central America) wrote about the beauty and variety of exotic flowers that grew there. These discoveries inspired a French **botanical** painter called Jacques Le Moyne de Morgues to make the long and dangerous journey by ship to the Floridas in 1564. Le Morgues kept a journal of his impressions of the Native Americans, whose way of life was closely connected with nature. Twenty years later, while living in England, de Morgues remembered his American experience in this painting.

A Pict as a Roman goddess

Le Morgues was fascinated by an early British tribe called the Picts, who painted their bodies in preparation for war. He portrayed a Pictish woman warrior to show that the British, like the Americans, had an ancient tribal history. Le Morgues painted the young woman as Flora, the Roman goddess of flowers. He covered her body with beautiful blossoms, many of which had recently been brought back to Europe by explorers from the New World.

Planning the picture

Le Morgues first planned the **composition** in pencil. Using water-colour, Le Morgues painted the clouds and the hills, and left the fort unpainted. He painted Flora's skin with **transparent** peach and the curves of her body with golden shading. Over this, Le Morgues drew detailed flowers.

Martin Johnson Heade (1819–1904) captured an orchid's beautiful curves in an oil painting based on drawings he made during an expedition to South America in the 1860s.

11

FLOWERS, ANIMALS, AND INSECTS, about 1670
Abraham Mignon, Dutch (1640–79), oil on canvas, 71 x 58.5 cm

Flower painting was an important art form during the seventeenth century in the Netherlands. Painters who usually painted religious art for churches searched for new **patrons**. During this time, wealthy middle class bankers and merchants started to collect paintings of nature to decorate their homes and they became the new patrons of art.

Full of life

In a sheltered glade, a clump of wildflowers almost hides a snake about to attack a field mouse. The forest teems with animals and plants in various stages of life. Mignon created the effect of strong sunlight creeping in from the left of the painting by **silhouetting** a clump of mushrooms that frames the scene. By placing the light in the foreground (front), Mignon darkened the background (behind the subject) to focus our attention on the drama about to unfold.

In this detail we can see how Abraham Mignon contrasted the innocent beauty of an ox-eye daisy with the deadly menace of a snake ready to strike.

Painting details

To achieve the almost microscopic detail in this picture, Mignon gradually built up the image in thin layers of paint that allowed him to work slowly and carefully. First he covered the entire scene in golden umber (brown). He then blended blue with green for the foliage to **contrast** with the warm umber that shines through the painting.

EGRET AND MALLOW PLANTS, date unknown, Yamamoto Baiitsu, Japanese (1783–1856), ink on silk, 182.5 x 53.5 cm

Yamamoto Baiitsu lived during a time when Japanese merchants were wealthier than the warlords who governed them. The middle classes were banned from political life, so they built lavish homes to show off their success. To show that they were not just rich but also educated, they **commissioned** artists to make beautiful paintings on silk scrolls.

In this landscape with flowers, Baiitsu drew the great variety of natural forms he saw at the edge of a marsh. He created a wide range of autumnal colours by diluting a brown-toned ink, called sumi, with water for the palest shades and painting with a nearly dry brush in the dark areas. Baiitsu first covered the mallow flowers in **opaque** white paint over the golden silk background. With a fine brush he then drew the delicate pink blossoms, letting some white show through to separate the petals from each other.

Balancing the composition

Baiitsu balanced the snowy white bird and the cliff with grasses and foliage. The horizontal shapes of the pond, a sweeping arc of sea grass, and the bird's long bill complement the strong vertical shapes of the bird's pencil-thin leg, the tall branch of mallow, and the shape of the scroll itself.

This detail shows Baiitsu's skill in creating a variety of shades and textures from only three colours: pink, white, and brownish black.

SPRING BOUQUET, 1866, Pierre-Auguste Renoir,
French (1841–1919), oil on canvas, 103.5 x 80 cm

Pierre-Auguste Renoir began his painting career as an artist who decorated expensive porcelain vases, but he soon realized that he was wasting his talent. In 1862, Renoir enrolled in the famous art school, Ecole Impériale et Spéciale des Beaux-Arts, in Paris, France. His friend and fellow student Jules Le Coeur introduced Renoir to his brother Charles, a well-known architect who commissioned this beautiful painting.

Painting shadows

Renoir had noticed that shadows are never black in hazy outdoor light. Instead they take on the colours of nearby objects. The white flowers in this bouquet cast light blue shadows that reflect the colour of the sky. Renoir exaggerated this effect so that his bouquet of flowers seems to be lit from within.

Thick and thin paint

Renoir created a feast of **textures** by using thin and thick layers of paint. He painted the ruffled petals of the peonies with rose and mauve mixed with white paint made thinner with **turpentine**. For the lilacs, Renoir painted a blur of transparent blue over the green **tone** of the leaves. He then made hundreds of lavender blossoms with tiny touches of paint. Renoir created a feeling of depth in the bouquet by using cool green colours for the foliage, which seem more distant than the warm yellows and whites in the flowers.

Using large brushes and thickly applied patches of yellow, blue, and green paint, Renoir put dappled sunlight around the flowers. The bold, textured surface of the background makes the bouquet of flowers seem more fragile.

PINKS AND CLEMATIS IN A CRYSTAL VASE, 1882
Edouard Manet, French (1832–83), oil on canvas, 55 x 33.5 cm

In 1882 an illness that would soon end his life forced Edouard Manet to move to the country for rest. His Parisian friends made frequent visits and brought bouquets of flowers. Because he was only able to work for short periods of time, Manet painted flowers. He captured the beauty of these cut flowers with the same attention that he had given to portraits of women before his illness.

Painting petals
Manet made the clematis with broad strokes of violet paint touched with a deeper shade of violet. Manet blended shades of pink and red paint for the carnations and added touches of white to define their petals. Manet shaped the leaves in masses of bluish green and used the wooden end of a brush to scratch lines on the wet paint to show the veins of the leaves.

Watery reflections
Manet painted the glass vase with bold deliberate strokes of transparent grey and **cerulean** blue. With tones of golden copper and white on the glass and water, he created reflections that distort the shape of the stems. As in many of his portraits, Manet left the background plain in order to focus our attention on the subject.

A rose bush set against a dark background complements this woman's beauty in a portrait by William Thorne (1863–1956).

19

WILD ROSES AND IRISES, 1887, John La Farge,
American (1835–1910), water-colour on paper, 31 x 25 cm

John La Farge became an artist during America's 'Gilded Age' in the late nineteenth century. This was a time when people who had made fortunes building railways and steel mills used their wealth to build universities and libraries. They used the finest architects to design new buildings and the best artists to decorate them. In 1876, La Farge, already an acclaimed painter, became one of the most popular designers of **murals** and stained glass windows.

A favourite subject
During the 1870s La Farge began painting water-colours of flowers. These paintings clearly show his enjoyment of nature and of water-colour paint.

Learning from Japanese art
By studying Japanese art, La Farge found a new way of drawing objects in space. He painted a flat green background to focus attention on the flowers. By cutting off the irises at the edge of the paper, he makes them seem nearer to the viewer and more distant from the greenery in the background.

Katsushika Hokusai (1760–1849) carefully designed the spaces between the irises and the leaves to show the air, which is as much a part of nature as plants and animals.

La Farge used transparent and opaque water-colour paint to show the delicacy of the blossoms and the powerful stems. He blended blue and indigo on wet paper to draw the petals. By leaving areas of paper unpainted, La Farge imitated sunlight shining through the delicate flowers.

231

SUNFLOWERS, 1889
Vincent van Gogh, Dutch (1853–90), oil on canvas, 92.5 x 71 cm

Vincent van Gogh moved from Holland to Paris, France, in 1884. After two years, van Gogh felt exhausted by the late nights spent in cafés drinking and talking with other painters. He moved to Arles, in the south of France, where he could paint outdoors in the warm and brilliant sunshine.

Indoors and outdoors

Landscape painting was van Gogh's first interest. But when the weather was bad he drew still-life pictures in his studio. This was an ideal way for van Gogh to study colours—in this painting of sunflowers, he studied the way bright shades of yellow appear to change when they are placed next to each other. Van Gogh knew that the yellows of the background and the foreground of the flowers would make all the brilliant yellows look less intense than they actually are and so create a peaceful effect.

Pure colours

Van Gogh avoided shading so that his colours would look brighter. He painted the round seed heads of the sunflowers with thick yellow paint dotted into the orange while it was still wet.

Van Gogh studied the jagged shapes of dried sunflowers in this oil painting of 1887.

BLUE LILY, about 1908
Piet Mondrian, Dutch (1872–1944), graphite and water-colour on paper, 26 x 17 cm

*P*iet Mondrian is famous for his **abstract** paintings: precise grids in black, white and primary colours. But before he began to paint in an abstract way Mondrian was inspired by nature.

Before and after

Before he painted this picture, Mondrian made careful drawings to study a freshly cut lily's construction and to watch the way it changed after he put it in water.

Using thin paints

Mondrian made the flower look almost transparent with thinly diluted yellow, blue and purple water-colour paints. First, he sketched out the composition exactly as he wanted the flower to look on the page. Mondrian then wet the paper and spread golden yellow paint over the background, brushing the colour up to the outline of the flower and stem. While the paper was still damp, he painted the lily a pale, watery blue, leaving areas of white paper uncovered to give the effect of light gleaming through the blossom. Dots of red painted on to the damp paper spread to look like the petals' bleeding marks.

*Georges Braque (1892–1963) used an inky black border to emphasize the geometric shapes in the background of this colour **etching**.*

24

P MONDRIAN

PORTRAIT OF MÄDA PRIMAVESI, about 1912–13
Gustav Klimt, Austrian (1862–1918), oil on canvas, 147 x 108 cm

Gustav Klimt began his career while he was still a student at the School of Applied Arts in Vienna, Austria. Klimt, his brother Ernst, and a fellow student were chosen by a teacher to help produce stained glass windows for a new church. The three young artists then opened a workshop in which they created murals and decorations for public buildings. As he became well known, Klimt attracted a circle of wealthy patrons, including Otto Primavesi, who commissioned this **portrait** of his daughter Mäda.

Salvador Dalí (1904–1989) made the flowers and butterflies cast large shadows against the rocks, making the woman on the cliff seem small by comparison.

A world of flowers

Klimt put the lovely ten-year-old girl in a floral fairyland. He created a puzzling space that can be seen as a landscape or a living room. The ground might be a garden path or a flower-patterned carpet. Klimt painted Mäda from below to make her seem larger. He creates a dreamy mood by contrasting her realistic figure with the abstract background.

Two techniques

Klimt focuses attention on Mäda by combining two painting **techniques**. Using fine brushes, he drew Mäda's face with delicate shading; for the floral background, Klimt used large brushes and thick swirls of paint that dance across the canvas. Mäda's dress gleams with bold brushstrokes of yellow, blue and mauve painted into a wet layer of white paint.

BLUE WATER LILIES, about 1916–19
Claude Monet, French (1840–1926), oil on canvas, 195 x 196 cm

In 1883, Claude Monet moved to Giverny, France where he built a lily pond. This pond gradually became one of the main subjects of his work. Monet wrote to a friend: "I'm absorbed in work. These landscapes showing water and reflections have become an obsession ...I want to represent what I experience."

Painting sunlight and water

In this painting, Monet drew the surface of the pond lit by sunlight. The willow branches at the top and their reflections on the water at the bottom of the picture frame the painting with dark strands of green, umber, and black. Monet left areas of the canvas blank at the edges to imitate rays of light coming through the trees. He painted bright cerulean blue over deep blue-violet to show the reflections of the sky on the water. The thick paint is as lively as the water's rippled surface seen close-up.

Painting quickly

Because **aquatic** flowers close their petals at dusk, Monet painted very quickly to capture the late afternoon shadows on the water. He blended white paint into the blue-violet colour of the water to suggest mist in the background.

In the hundreds of water lily paintings and studies that Monet worked on between 1916 and 1926, he created an emotional way of painting that no other artist copied during his lifetime. In these paintings the act of painting and the rich, textured paint surface are important to Monet. The lily pond seems unimportant by comparison.

NIGHT FLOWERS, 1918, Paul Klee,
German (1879–1940), water-colour on paper, 17 x 16 cm

*a*s a child Paul Klee was fascinated by flowers and grew daisies in his own miniature garden. At ten, Klee kept a series of sketch-books dedicated to flowers.

A daisy or the sun?

In this imaginary scene, Klee created a simple, almost primitive, picture of flowers, trees, and ferns that might be the Garden of Eden. For Klee, the ordinary daisy, which often grows in bad soil, symbolized the determination of plants to survive. With its simple arrangement of white petals around a yellow centre, the daisy looks like the sun—the source of life for plants.

A garden of the imagination

Klee did not draw a garden using the technique of **perspective**.

By putting green paint on top of white paint, Klee created the magic of moonlight shining through daisy petals.

Intense, warm colours, like red, look closer to the viewer than pale, cool colours, like blue. So Klee made the red tower in the foreground and the pale blue fir tree in the background seem a long way apart using colour. In contrast to the pink cloud-like shapes that frame the scene on two sides, the soft blue background seems as far away as a distant galaxy.

Large and small evergreen trees float through the landscape and the red tower suggests that humans are somewhere in Klee's garden.

WHITE SWEET PEAS, 1926, Georgia O'Keeffe,
American (1887–1986), **pastel** on paper, 62.5 x 47.5 cm

In the 1920s, Georgia O'Keeffe spent her winters in New York City. Looking out of her twenty-eighth-floor studio she painted pictures of skyscrapers being built. Although O'Keeffe admired these huge modern buildings, she felt cut off from nature and so she began to paint flowers. O'Keeffe wrote: "When you take a flower into your hands and really look at it, it's your world for the moment. I want to give that world to someone else." In this painting of sweet peas, O'Keeffe showed the viewer the world of flowers by painting a flower close-up.

Working from memory

The freshness of O'Keeffe's colours is a result of her approach to painting. O'Keeffe tried to remember all the flowers she had seen before. After she had a clear image in her mind of shapes, textures and colours, she began to paint. O'Keeffe never changed her mind and never made corrections that might have made the colours more dull.

A paintbrush and pastels

O'Keeffe drew this picture with pastels — sticks of soft coloured chalk. Starting with white, the brightest colour in her **palette**, she blended bright turquoise and yellow for the petals. As shading she used a cool mauve pastel. She used a dry paintbrush to blend the pastels and make the gradual change in colour from white to mauve, as seen on the large flower at the left.

GERANIUM, about 1926
Charles Sheeler, American (1883–1965), oil on canvas, 80 x 65 cm

Charles Sheeler trained as an artist and later worked as a commercial photographer to support his family. He was fascinated by the ways in which photographs can change the appearance of objects. Sheeler used the reality and the illusions of photography in his paintings.

Grabbing attention

At first glance this painting seems to be a straightforward view of an ordinary flower. Sheeler lit the plant from behind and positioned it against a plain background to focus our attention on the single red flower. He cut off the image at the edge as if the picture was a badly taken photograph.

Different viewpoints

Sheeler used several points of view in his composition. We see the geranium straight on, but the table and chair are drawn as if they are seen from above. Sheeler tilted the table so that the plant is pushed forward in space.

Sheeler worked with two different painting techniques. He used fine brushes to carefully draw the geranium and the chair. He painted the background with big brushes to create a soft-focus impression of light.

Joseph Stella (1877–1946) drew this picture with a sharp silver rod on specially prepared paper. The silver 'pen' left tiny bits of metal on the paper which turned black with time.

THE PURPLE ROBE, 1937
Henri Matisse, French (1869–1954), oil on canvas, 71 x 58.5 cm

In the mid-1930s, economic depression and the threat of another war in Europe made Henri Matisse feel worried. He moved back to Paris from the south of France, where he had begun to feel isolated, and filled his studio with flowers, wall hangings, and exotic birds that reminded him of a visit he had made to Tahiti (in Polynesia).

Straight lines and wavy lines

Matisse painted the subject of a picture (in this case, a woman and her flowers) and the background in the same way. He repeated the curves of the stems in the vase in the flowing stripes of the woman's purple gown and in the wavy white lines of the curtain. The designs on the table and on the woman's skirt are shaped like flowers. The curved lines and patterns in the painting are balanced by straight lines on the carpet, the wallpaper and the tiled floor.

Henri Matisse varied the thickness of the lines in this lino cut to create different shades of white.

Bright and black

Although Matisse used bright shades of red and yellow in the flowers and in the background, he gave the picture a peaceful mood through the large areas of clear blue-green paint. Matisse defined the edges of the room and gave a feeling of depth to the flat picture with a strip of black in the bottom left-hand corner of the canvas.

36

THE FLOWER VENDOR, 1941
Diego Rivera, Mexican (1886–1957), oil on canvas, 120 x 120 cm

In 1907, Diego Rivera moved from Mexico to Europe to study painting. For fourteen years the gifted young artist absorbed the influence of the artists **Pablo Picasso** (1881-1973) and **Joan Miró** (1893-1983). When he returned to his own country Rivera created his own powerful, distinctive painting style. He studied Mexican history, art and culture and used it as inspiration for his art.

Huge flowers

In this painting of an Aztec woman with flowers, Rivera created an image that has the impact of an ancient stone carving. Using bold, simple shapes, he emphasized the woman's grace as she gently places an enormous mass of calla lilies on the ground. Rivera enlarged the flowers so that they almost fill the square canvas to the edges. The dark background creates a frame that draws attention to the lilies, which Rivera painted in delicate tints of green, yellow, and white.

Rivera created a feeling of depth through the shapes of the flowers. The petals and stems are shown head on in the centre of the picture. Closer to the edges, the petals are seen in **profile** and the stems curve into the distance.

Rivera signed his name on a little note card in the bottom left-hnd corner. This is a tradition in Mexican folk painting.

Rivera paint masses of marigolds. Marigolds are displayed during the Aztec Day of the Dead celebration.

THE FLOWER BARGE, 1954
André Bauchant, French (1873–1958), oil on canvas, 70 x 96 cm

André Bauchant left school at the age of fourteen to work in his father's nursery garden. Although his education was brief, Bauchant continued to enjoy reading history and mythology. Later, when he was in the army, Bauchant told these stories of great events and legendary feats to his friends to escape the boredom of military life. When he was released from the army in 1920, Bauchant began painting pictures inspired by these mythological stories.

A bouquet, or a boat, or both?

Bauchant used diferent **scales** to great effect in his picture of a barge overflowing with flowers. The buildings, trees, and the boat are in proportion to the vine-covered wall and bouquets in the foreground. But the enormous blossoms in the barge seem to be bigger than the boat itself. We can also see the flower barge as a bouquet that is in perfect proportion to the wall and the bouquets in the foreground.

Detailed and bright

Bauchant wanted to paint his ideas exactly as he had imagined them,

A little bouquet stands to attention for the arrival of Bauchant's flower barge.

so he showed everything in minute detail. The little house in the distance is drawn in as much detail as the flowers in the foreground. He kept his colours pure throughout, rather than making the colours in the background softer, which is a method often used by painters to give their paintings a feeling of depth.

40

THE WRESTLERS' TOMB, 1960
René Magritte, Belgian (1898–1967), oil on canvas, 95 x 127.5 cm

René Magritte thought that his dreams revealed the hidden meaning of ordinary objects. Magritte called himself a painter, not an artist, because he was not interested in just drawing beautiful things. He wanted to draw a world of ideas.

A huge rose or a small room?

Magritte enlarged this rose to remind us of how the smell of flowers can take over a whole room. What we cannot tell is whether Magritte has painted a large rose in a small room, or a normal rose in a tiny room. By creating a picture that is also a puzzle, Magritte forces us to think in a different way.

A different way of looking at the world

Magritte made this picture by using a precise, realistic, painting style. He copied an advertising photograph in order to reproduce the rose's perfectly formed petals. With fine brushes, Magritte blended shades of bright red paint, without leaving any brush marks that might reveal the touch of an artist's hand on the surface of the canvas. He painted the room in toned-down shades of red and brown that set off the brilliant flower. Although the window lets in natural light, Magritte put harsh artificial light from an unseen source in front of the painting to make dark shadows that almost push the flower out of the picture frame.

Magritte thought that most people went through life without thinking. In this unsettling picture, Magritte makes us think again about what a flower is.

CAMELLIAS, 1991, Robert Kushner,
American (born 1949), oil and gold leaf on canvas, 180 x 90 cm

As a child in southern California, Robert Kushner played in a back garden filled with flowers. One of his earliest memories was of escaping to the garden next door to smell the perfume of the camellias. The sheer beauty of the flowers of his childhood later inspired Kushner in his paintings.

His painting *Camellias* not only celebrates the beauty of the flowers but also shows a knowledge of eighteenth-century Japanese painting. Early Japanese artists painted backgrounds of gold leaf to reflect the light and create a mood of splendour. Kushner used the traditional materials and methods of Japanese painting to create a different version of this type of painting.

Planning the painting

Kushner first made a series of drawings of the camellias as a way of planning the composition. Like Japanese painters, Kushner worked with the canvas flat on the floor in order to control the flow of paint from his brush and avoid paint drips. Kushner drew the outlines of flowers and leaves using long, flexible brushes. He then painted a background of varying textures. After the paint was dry he put squares of **gold leaf** over half the background. The gleaming gold squares make up a grid rather like the shape of the two square canvases that make up the painting.

*The sharp details of the monarch butterfly contrast with the blurred roses in the background. This is the super-realistic style of **contemporary** artist Audrey Flack (born 1931).*

Glossary and Index

ABSTRACT: a picture or sculpture which has shape and colour but no recognizable subject.

AQUATIC: anything living in water.

AZTEC: descended from the Aztec people of Central Mexico.

BOTANICAL: anything to do with plants.

CERULEAN: the name given to the colour dark sky-blue.

COLOUR: when it is used by painters three different terms are used for colours.

The actual appearance of the colour (red, blue, bluish green, etc.) is called its hue.

A lighter or darker version of a hue is created by adding white or black and is called a shade.

A hue can be changed by adding a small amount of another colour and this is called a tint. For example, a painter might add a small amount of red to grey, to yellow, and to blue and create reddish tints of these original colours.

COMMISSION: a work of art produced for a **patron**.

COMPOSITION: the arrangement of objects, figures, colours and shapes in a painting.

CONTEMPORARY: of the same period in time.

CONTRAST: the differences in light and dark, shapes and colours.

ETCHING: scratch an image on to a metal plate, dip it in acid to define the image, cover it with ink and press it on to paper to print an etching.

GOUACHE: an **opaque** form of water-colour, which is also called tempera or body colour.

GOLD LEAF: squares of real gold that are pounded thinner than paper. Gold leaf is placed on to a surface coated with glue and carefully pressed into position with soft cotton.

MIRO, JOAN (1893-1983): a Spanish semi-**abstract** artist who was very influential because of his use of colours.

MURAL: a large painting on a wall.

OPAQUE: something which does not let light pass through it. Opaque paints hide what is under them. (The opposite of TRANSPARENT).

PALETTE: the name of the board an artist mixes paint on.

PASTEL: a soft crayon made of powdered pigment (colour), chalk, and water mixed with gum to form a stick.

PATRON: an individual, or organization, that supports the arts or an individual artist.

PERSPECTIVE: a method of drawing people, places, and things to make them appear solid or three-dimensional rather than flat. Six basic rules of perspective are used in Western art.

1. People in a painting appear larger when they are near to the viewer and gradually become smaller as they get further away.

2. People in the foreground overlap the people or objects behind them.

3. People get closer together as they get further away.

4. People in the distance are closer to the top of the picture than those in the foreground.

5. Colours are brighter and shadows are stronger in the foreground. Colours and shadows are paler and softer in the background.

6. Lines that in real life are parallel (such as the line of a ceiling and the line of a floor) are drawn at an angle, and the lines meet at the horizon line, which is the line that represents the eye level of the artist and the viewer.

PICASSO, PABLO (1881-1973): the most famous artist of this century and one of the most influential. He was born in Spain but moved to Paris in 1904. He was not only a painter, he was also a sculptor, a potter and a designer.

PORTRAIT: a painting, drawing, sculpture, or photograph that represents an individual's appearance and, usually, his or her personality.

PROFILE: seen from the side.

RENAISSANCE: the period of European history from the early fifteenth to the mid-sixteenth centuries. Renaissance means 'rebirth' in French and marks the change from the Middle Ages to the Modern Age. The rebirth refers to the revival of arts, literature, politics, trade, sciences and medicine.

SCALE: the size of an object compared with a human figure. For example: in a painting of a mountain, we can only judge the mountain's size if we compare it with a human figure.

SILHOUETTE: an image, such as a **portrait**, that consists of the outline of its shape in a solid colour.

STILL LIFE: a painting, drawing, or photograph whose main subject is an object or a group of objects.

SYMBOLIC: an image that represents something other than itself.

TECHNIQUE: the process or practice that is used to obtain a particular artistic effect.

TEXTURE: the surface quality of a painting. For example, an oil painting could have a thin, smooth surface texture or a thick, rough surface texture.

TONE: the overall colour of a painting. For example, an artist might begin by painting the entire picture in shades of greenish grey. After more colours are added using **transparent** shadows and highlights, the mass of greenish grey colour underneath will show through and create an even tone. *See also* COLOUR.

TRANSPARENT: something which allows light to pass through it. A transparent colour allows colours underneath it to be seen. (The opposite of OPAQUE).

TROMPE L'OEIL: the name given to the **technique** where an artist paints a scene so realistically that the viewer is tricked into thinking that the people and the objects in the picture are real. See also PERSPECTIVE.
TURPENTINE: a strong-smelling liquid made from pine sap.

VELLUM: very thin goat's skin.

abstract, 24
Arcimboldo, Giuseppe, 8

Baiitsu, Yamamoto, 14
Bauchant, André, 40
Blue Lily, 25
Blue Water Lilies, 29

Camellias, 45
commission, 14, 16
composition, 10, 24, 34, 44

Egret and Mallow Plants, 15

Flower Barge, The, 41
Flowers, Animals, and Insects, 13
Flower Vendor, The, 39

Geranium, 35
Gogh, Vincent van, 22

Klee, Paul, 30
Klimt, Gustav, 26

La Farge, John, 20

Magritte, René, 42
Manet, Edouard, 18
Matisse, Henri, 36
Mignon, Abraham, 12
Mondrian, Piet, 24
Monet, Claude, 28
Morgues, Jacques Le Moyne de, 10

Night Flowers, 31

O'Keeffe, Georgia, 32
opaque, 14, 20

perspective, 30, 32
Picasso, Pablo, 38
Pinks and Clematis in a Crystal Vase, 19
Portrait of Mäda Primavesi, 27
Purple Robe, The, 37

Renoir, Pierre-Auguste, 16
Rivera, Diego, 38

Sheeler, Charles, 34
Spring, 9
Spring Bouquet, 17
Still life, 12, 16, 32
Sunflowers, 23

texture, 16
tone, 16, 18
transparent, 10, 16, 18, 20

White Sweet Peas, 33
Wild Roses and Irises, 21
Wrestlers' Tomb, The, 43

Young Daughter of the Picts, A, 11

Credits

Frontispiece

THE WHITE HERON, 1918–20
Joseph Stella, American (1877–1964)
Oil on canvas, 120 x 72.5 cm
Yale University Art Gallery, New Haven, Connecticut 1941.691

Page

9   *SPRING*, 1573
Giuseppe Arcimboldo, Italian, Musée de Louvre © Photo R.M.N.

10 *STILL LIFE WITH CATTELAYA, TWO HUMMINGBIRDS, AND BEETLE,*
Martin Johnson Heade, American
Oil on canvas, 35 x 55 cm (detail)
Private Collection

11 *A YOUNG DAUGHTER OF THE PICTS*, c.1585
Jacques Le Moyne de Morgues, French
Yale Center for British Art, New Haven, Connecticut
Paul Mellon Collection

13 *FLOWERS, ANIMALS, AND INSECTS*, c. 1670
Abraham Mignon, Dutch
Musées Royaux des Beaux–Arts de Belgique, Brussels

15 *EGRET AND MALLOW PLANTS*, Edo Period, date unknown
Yamamoto Baiitsu, Japanese
Courtesy Dr. & Mrs. Kurt Gitter, New Orleans

17 *SPRING BOUQUET*, 1866
Pierre–Auguste Renoir, French
Fogg Art Museum, Cambridge, Massachusetts
Harvard University Art Museums
Bequest of Grenville L. Winthrop

18 *WOMAN IN KIMONO*, 1892, (detail)
William Thorn, American (1863–1956)
Oil on canvas, 88 x 28 cm
Courtesy ACA Gallery, New York

19 *PINKS AND CLEMATIS IN A CRYSTAL VASE*, 1882
Edouard Manet, French
Musée D'Orsay © Photo R.M.N.

20 *IRISES*, c.1822
Katsushika Hokusai, Japanese (1760–1849)
Print 23.5 x 35 cm
The Metropolitan Museum of Art, New York
Frederick Charles Hewitt Bequest Fund, 1912

21 *WILD ROSES AND IRISES*, 1887
John La Farge, American
The Metropolitan Museum of Art, New York
Gift of Priscilla A.B. Henderson in memory of her grandfather, Russell St. Sturgis, a founder of the Metropolitan Museum

22 *SUNFLOWERS*, 1887
Vincent van Gogh, Dutch
Oil on canvas, 42.5 x 60 cm
The Metropolitan Museum of Art, New York
Rogers Fund, 1949

23 *SUNFLOWERS*, 1889
Vincent van Gogh, Dutch
The Metropolitan Museum of Art, New York
Rogers Fund, 1949. (49.41.)

25 *BLUE LILY*, c. 1908
Piet Mondrian, Dutch
Courtesy Sidney Janis Gallery, New York

26 *THE LORELEI*, 1948
Salvador Dali, Spanish
Water-colour on paper
Courtesy Mrs. Albert D. Lasker

27 *PORTRAIT OF MÄDA PRIMAVESI*, c. 1912–13
Gustav Klimt, Austrian
The Metropolitan Museum of Art, New York
Gift of Andre and Clara Mertens, in memory of her mother Jenny Pulitzer Steiner, 1964. (64.148.)

29 *BLUE WATER LILLIES*, c. 1916–19
Claude Monet, French
Musée D'Orsay © Photo R.M.N. SPADEM

31 *NIGHT FLOWERS*, 1918
Paul Klee, German
Museum Folkwang, Essen

33 *WHITE SWEET PEAS*, 1926
Georgia O'Keeffe, American
Private Collection

34 *YELLOW LOTUS*, 1920
Joseph Stella, American (1877–1946)
Silverpoint and crayon on paper, 17.5 x 26 cm
Collection of Mr. and Mrs. Eric P. Widing
Courtesy Richard York Gallery, New York

35 *GERANIUM*, c. 1926
Charles Sheeler, American
Collection of Whitney Museum of American Art, New York
Gift of Gertrude Vanderbilt Whitney 31.343.

36 *THE BASKET OF FLOWERS*, 1917
Georges Braque, French
Courtesy Hubert Gallery, New York

36 *BASKET OF BEGONIAS*, 1938
Henri Matisse, French
Courtesy Isselbacher Gallery, New York

37 *PURPLE ROBE AND ANEMONES*, 1937
Henri Matisse, French
The Baltimore Museum of Art: The Cone Collection, formed by Dr. Claribel Cone and Miss Etta Cone of Baltimore, Maryland, (BMA 1950.261.)

38 *WOMAN WITH MARIGOLDS*, 1954
Diego Rivera, Mexican
Water-colour on paper, 37.5 x 27.5 cm
Courtesy Mary–Anne Martin/Fine Art, New York

39 *THE FLOWER VENDOR*, 1941
Diego Rivera, Mexican
Norton Simon Museum, Pasadena, California
(P. 1980.2.3.) Gift of Mr. Cary Grant, 1980

41 *THE FLOWER BOAT*, 1941
André Bauchant, French
Courtesy Mrs. Albert D. Lasker

43 *THE WRESTLER'S TOMB*, 1960
René Magritte, Belgian
© 1993 C. Herscovici / ARS, NY
Photo courtesy Mr. Harry Torczyner

44 *MONARCH AND ROSE*, 1980
Audrey Flack, American
Acrylic on paper 37.5 x 53 cm
Courtesy Louis K. Meisel Gallery, New York, Photo: Steve Lopez

45 *CAMELLIAS*, 1991
Robert Kushner, American
Courtesy Midtown Payson Gallery, New York